THE
VAN MORRISON
GUITAR SONGBOOK

EXCLUSIVELY DISTRIBUTED BY

HAL•LEONARD®

ISBN-13: 978-0-7390-5116-0

CONTENTS   ALBUM   PAGE

BROWN EYED GIRL

Words and Music by
VAN MORRISON

Moderately fast ♩ = 144

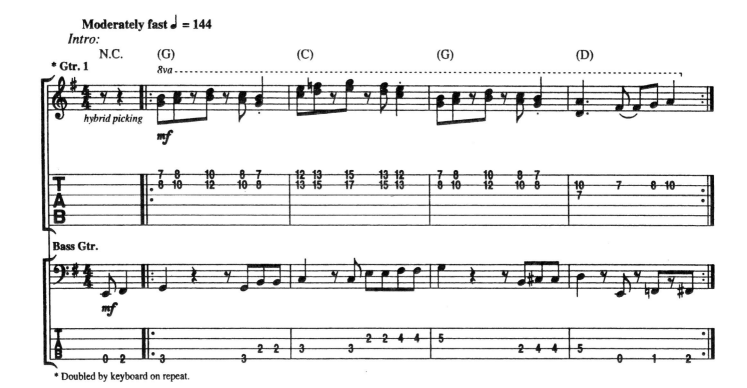

* Doubled by keyboard on repeat.

* Bass Gtr. continues simile.

Brown Eyed Girl - 9 - 1

4

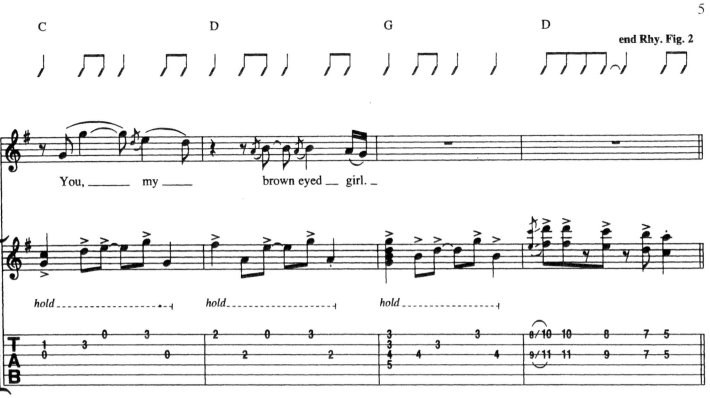

Verse 2:

* Keyboard arranged for guitar.

Go-ing down the old ___ mine ___ with a tran - sis - tor ra - di - o. ___

Stand - ing in the sun - light laugh-ing, ___ hid - ing be - hind ___ a rain-bow's wall. ___

Bridge:

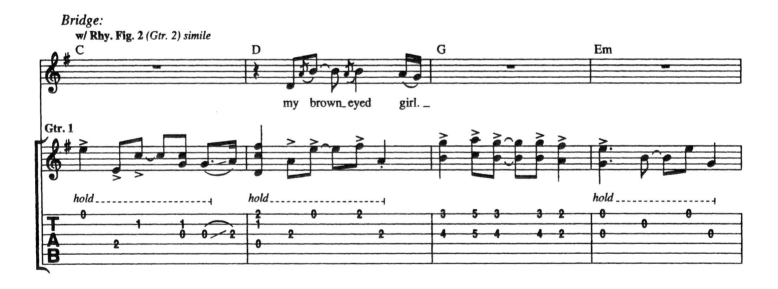

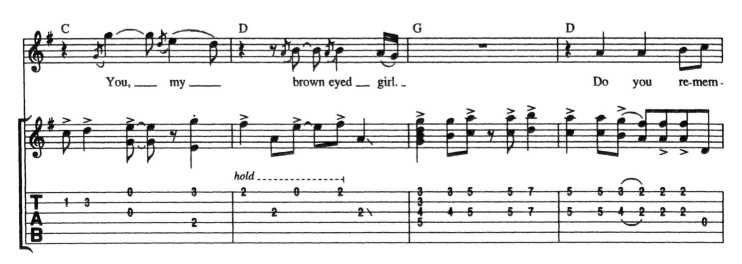

Brown Eyed Girl - 9 - 5

8

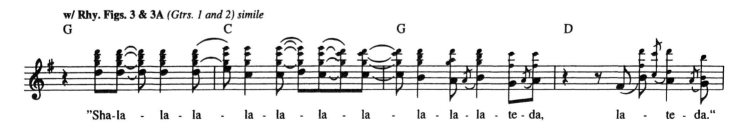

Do you re-mem-ber when   (a) we used to sing:

Out-Chorus:
w/ Rhy. Figs. 3 & 3A *(Gtrs. 1 and 2, 3 times) simile*

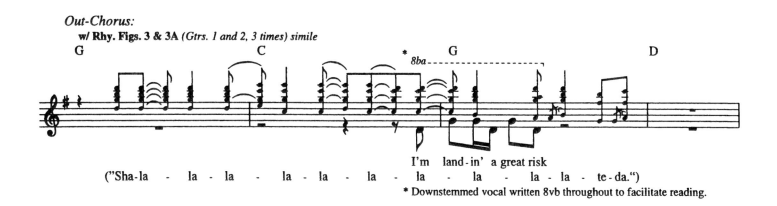

I'm land-in' a great risk
("Sha-la - la - la-la - la-la - la - la - la - la-te-da.")
* Downstemmed vocal written 8vb throughout to facilitate reading.

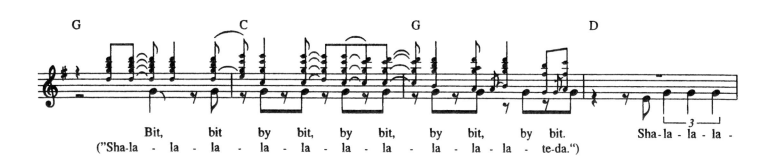

Bit,   bit   by   bit,   by   bit,   by   bit,   by bit.   Sha-la-la-la-
("Sha-la - la - la - la-la - la-la - la - la-la-te-da.")

Fade

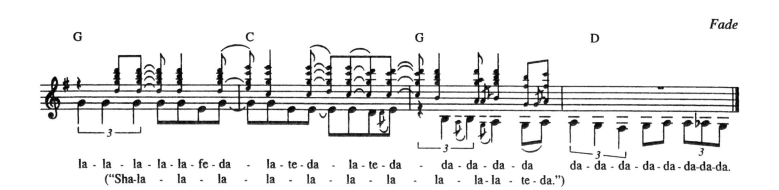

la-la - la-la-la-fe-da - la-te-da - la-te-da - da-da-da-da   da-da-da-da-da-da-da-da.
("Sha-la - la - la - la-la - la - la - la-la-te-da.")

AND IT STONED ME

Words and Music by
VAN MORRISON

Moderately slow ♩ = 80

Verse 1:

1. Half a mile from the coun-ty fair, _ and the rain _ come pour-in' down. _

Me and Bil-ly stand - in' there _ with a sil - ver half a crown. _

Hands are full of a fish-in' rod _ and the tack-le _____ on our backs.

We just stood _ there get-tin' wet __ with our backs a-gainst _ the fence.

Bridge:

Oh _____ the wa-ter, oh _____ the wa-ter,

* Two horns arranged for one guitar

And It Stoned Me - 10 - 1

14

Stoned me just like go-in' home, and it stoned me. 2. Then the

Verse 2:
w/ Rhy. Fig. 1, (Gtr. 1, 4 times)

rain let up, and the sun came up and we were get-tin' dry.

Al-most glad a pick-up truck near-ly passed us by. So we

jumped right in, and the dri - ver grinned _ and he dropped us up _ the road. _ And we

looked at the swim, and we jumped right _ in, not to men - tion _ fish-in' poles. _

* Piano arranged for gtr.

Verse 3:
  w/ Rhy. Fig. 1 simile, Gtrs. 1 & 3 (2 times)
  w/ Riff C (Gtr. 2)

way back home ___ we sang _ a song, . but our throats were get-tin' dry. ___ Then we

saw _ the man . from a-cross the road _ with the sun - shine in his eye. Well he lived_

all a-lone in his own _ lit-tle home _ with a great _ big _ gal-lon jar. _ There were

bot-tles, two, _____ one for me and you, _____ and he said, "Hey! ___ There _ you are!" ____

Bridge:
w/ Rhy. Fig. 2 (Gtr. 1)
w/ Riff B (Gtr. 2)
w/ Rhy. Fig. 4 (Gtr. 3, 2 times)

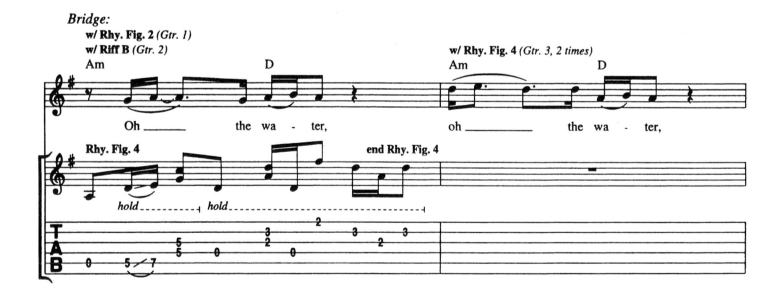

Oh _____ the wa - ter, oh _____ the wa - ter,

D.S. %% al Coda II

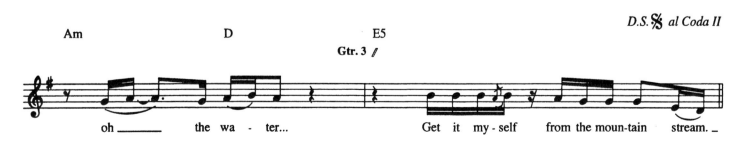

Gtr. 3 //

oh _____ the wa - ter... Get it my-self from the moun-tain stream. _

And It Stoned Me - 10 - 9

BLUE MONEY

Words and Music by
VAN MORRISON

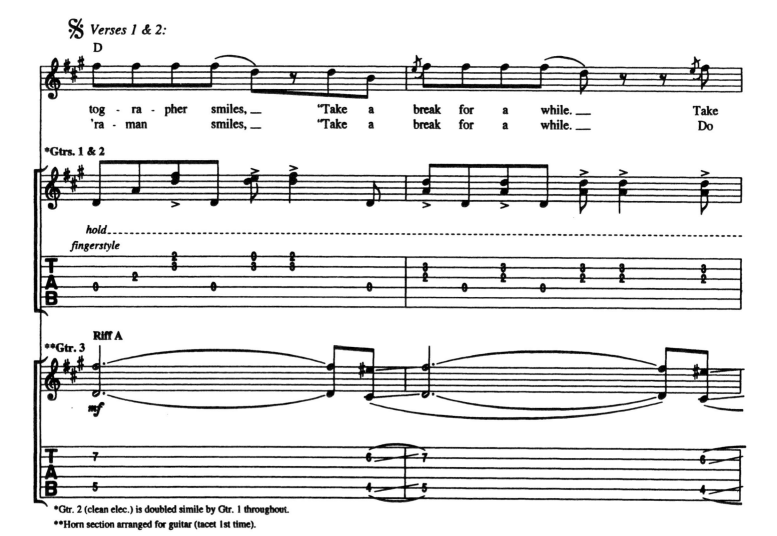

*Gtr. 2 (clean elec.) is doubled simile by Gtr. 1 throughout.

**Horn section arranged for guitar (tacet 1st time).

Blue Money - 10 - 1

*Second time only.

We'll go out and spend all of your.... (Blue mon-ey.) Blue

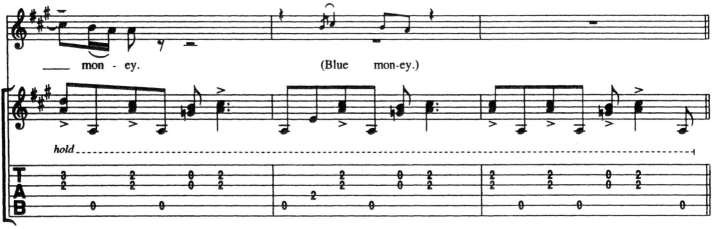

mon - ey. (Blue mon-ey.)

Do, do you do, _ do, do, do you do, _ do, do, do you do, _

26

do, do, do you do, ___ do da. Al - right.

(Do da.) Do da. Al -

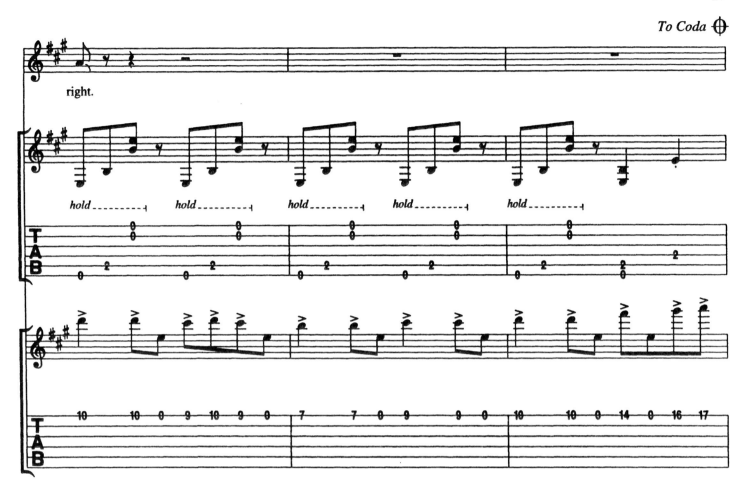

D.S. 𝄋 *al Coda*

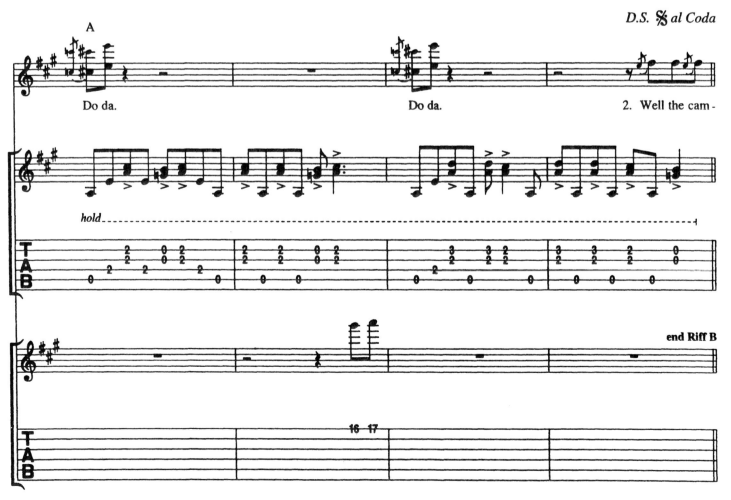

⊕ *Coda*

One more time. ___

Do, do you do, ___ do, do, do you do, ___

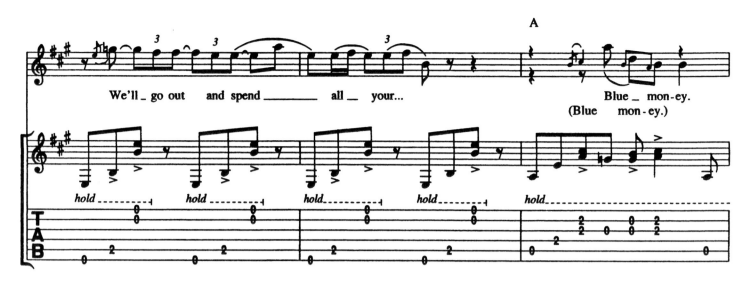

We'll _ go out and spend _____ all _ your...   Blue _ mon - ey.
(Blue mon - ey.)

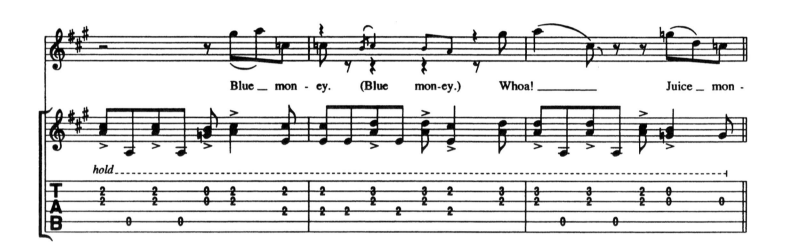

Blue _ mon - ey. (Blue mon - ey.) Whoa! _____ Juice _ mon -

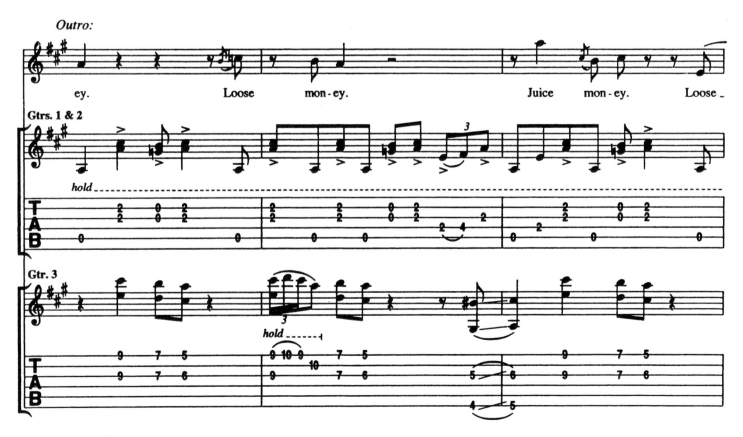

Outro:

ey.   Loose mon - ey.   Juice mon - ey. Loose _

mon-ey, hon-ey.
(Do, do, do.) (Do, do, do, do.)
What kind of mon-ey hon-ey?

*Repeat and Fade

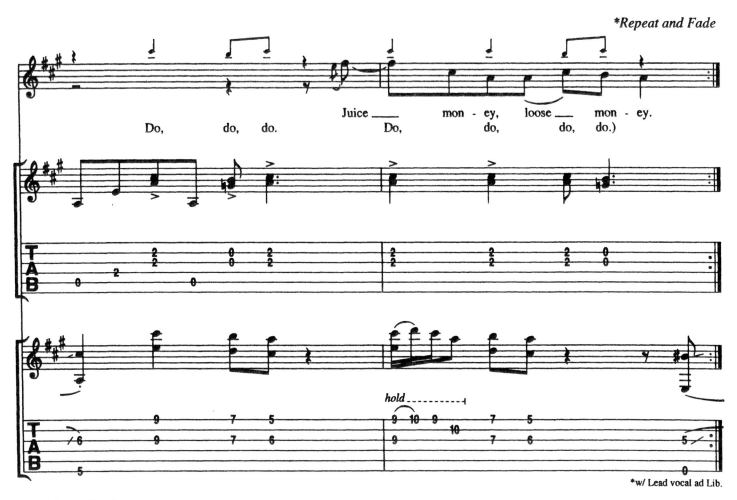

Do, do, do. Juice ___ mon - ey, loose ___ mon - ey.
Do, do, do, do.)

*w/ Lead vocal ad Lib.

Blue Money - 10 - 10

BRAND NEW DAY

Words and Music by
VAN MORRISON

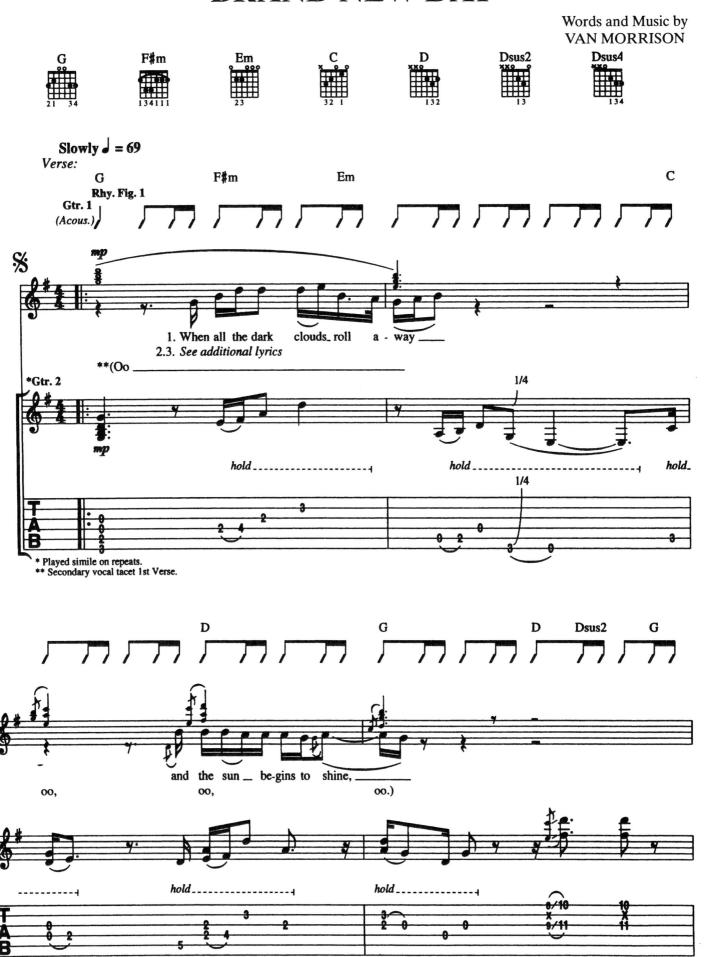

* Played simile on repeats.
** Secondary vocal tacet 1st Verse.

Brand New Day - 6 - 1

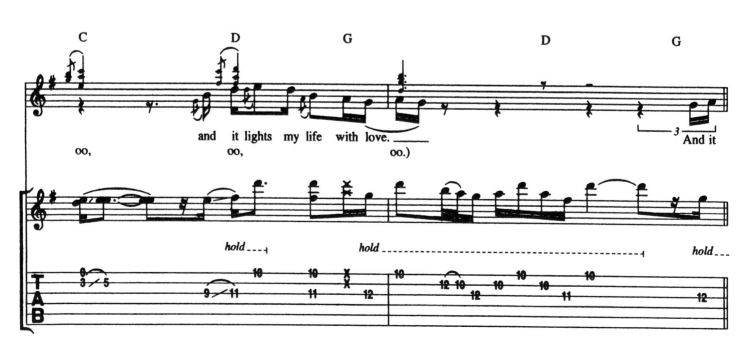

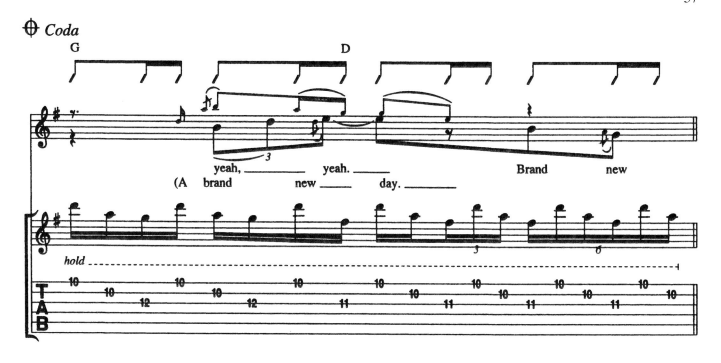

*w/ lead vocal ad Lib. till fade.

**Gtr. 2 played simile on repeats

Verse 2:

I was lost and double crossed

With my hands behind my back.

I was longtime hurt, and thrown in the dirt,

Shoved out on the railroad track.

I've been used, abused and so confused,

And I had nowhere to run.

But I stood and looked, and my eyes got hooked

On that beautiful morning sun.

(To Chorus:)

Verse 3:

And the sun shines down all on the ground,

Yeah, and the grass is oh so green,

And my heart is still and I've got the will

And I don't really feel so mean.

Here it comes, here it comes, here it comes right now.

And it comes right in on time.

Well it eases me, and it pleases me,

And it satisfies my mind.

(To Chorus:)

CARAVAN

Words and Music by
VAN MORRISON

* Piano arranged for guitar.
** Gtr. 1: Acoustic guitar; replaces Gtrs. 1 and 2: piano.

Caravan - 9 - 1

40

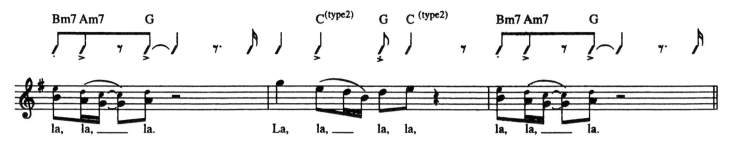

la, la, ____ la. La, la, ____ la, la, la, la, ____ la.

Verse:

And the car-a-van _ is paint-ed red and white, _ that means ev-'ry-bod-y's stay - ing

o - ver night. _ And the bare - foot gyp-sy play-er round the camp-fire _ sing and play, _

Chorus:

And a wom-an tells _ us of her _ ways. _ La, la, ____ la, la,

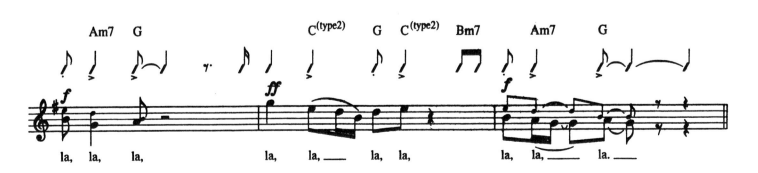

la, la, la, la, la, ____ la, la, la, la, ____ la. ____

* Bar at VII.

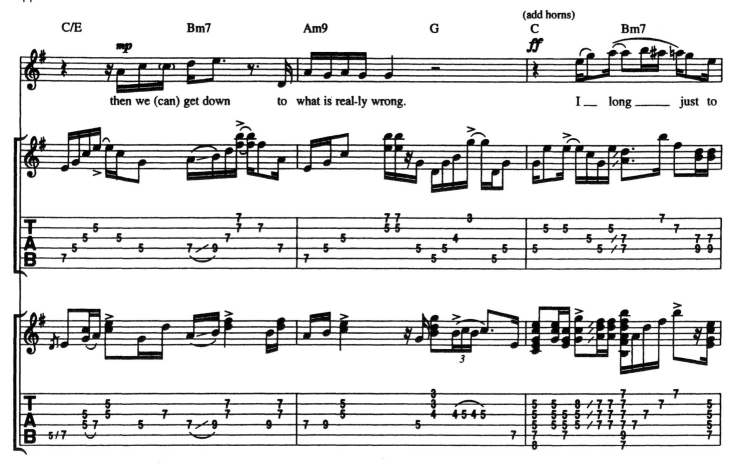

45

Sweet la - dy of the _____ night, _____ I shall _____

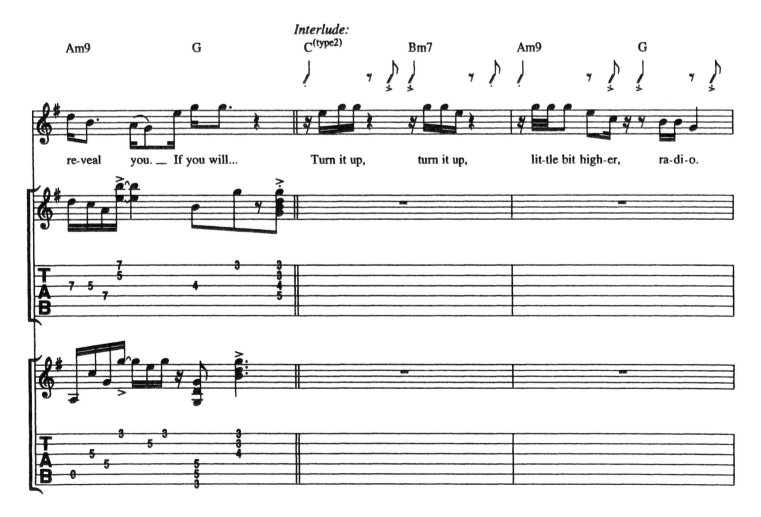

re-veal you. _ If you will... Turn it up, turn it up, lit-tle bit high-er, ra-di-o.

46

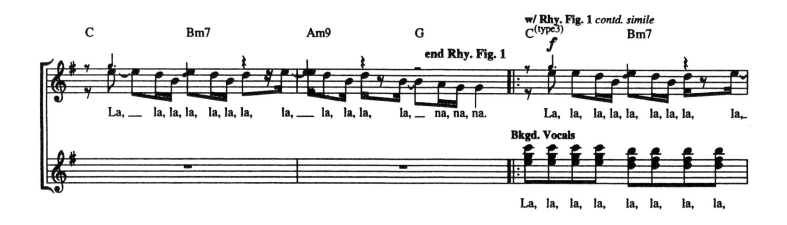

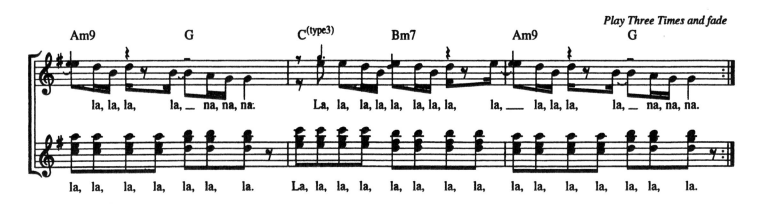

Caravan - 9 - 9

DOMINO

Words and Music by
VAN MORRISON

Domino - 5 - 1

48

50

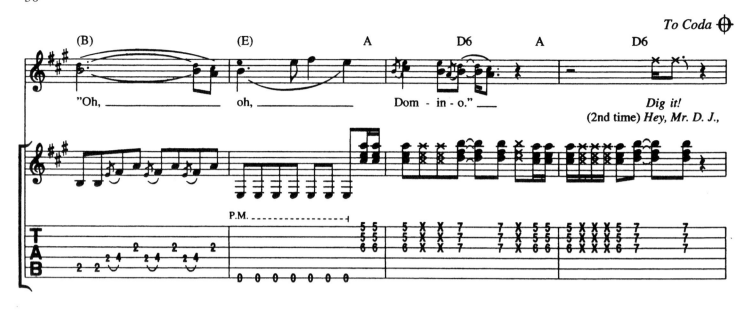

"Oh, _____ oh, _____ Dom - in - o." _____

Dig it!
(2nd time) *Hey, Mr. D. J.,*

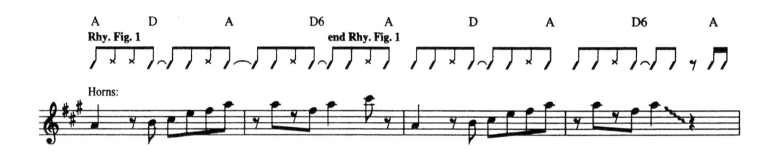

Horns:

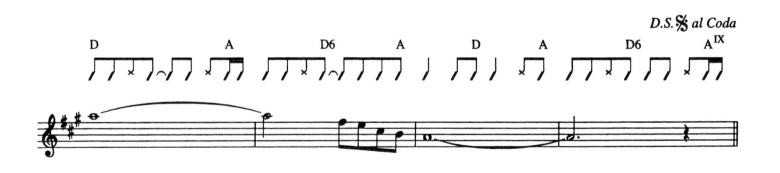

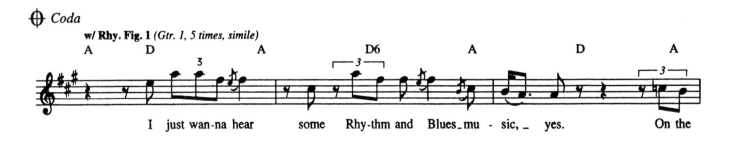

I just wan-na hear some Rhy-thm and Blues_mu - sic, _ yes. On the

ra - di - o.　On the ra - di - o.　on the ra - di - o.　Ah,　a - a - al -

right. Ah,　a - a - al - right. __　Ah,　a - a - al - right. __　Ah　ow. __　*Spoken: Hear the band.*

Outro:

Horns:

Verse 2:
There's no need for argument.
There's no argument at all.
And if you never hear from him,
That just means he didn't call.
Or vice-a-versa, that depends on wherever you're at.
Alright.
And if you never hear from me, that just means I would rather not.
(To Chorus:)

CRAZY LOVE

Words and Music by
VAN MORRISON

Moderately slow ♩ = 76

Verse 1:

1. I can hear her heart beat from a thou-sand miles, and the

* Played fingerstyle throughout   **Bass gtr. plays D.

heav-ens o-pen ev-'ry time she smiles. And when I come to her that's

where I be-long, yet I'm run-ning to her like a riv-er's song. She give me

Crazy Love - 8 - 1

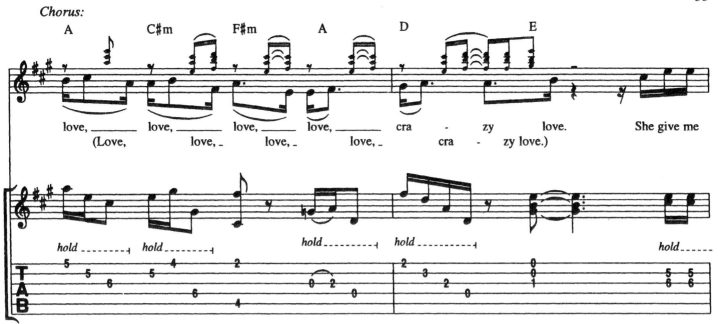

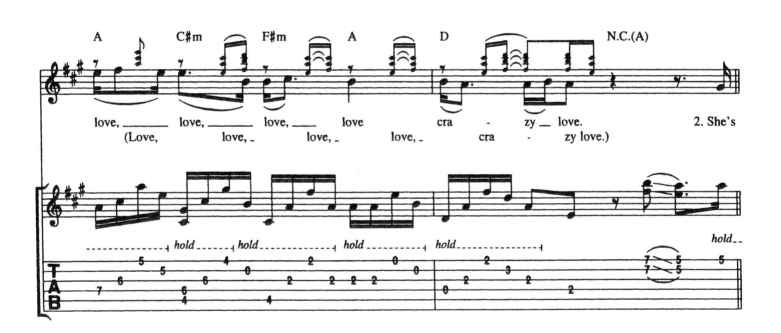

Verse 2:

Crazy Love - 8 - 2

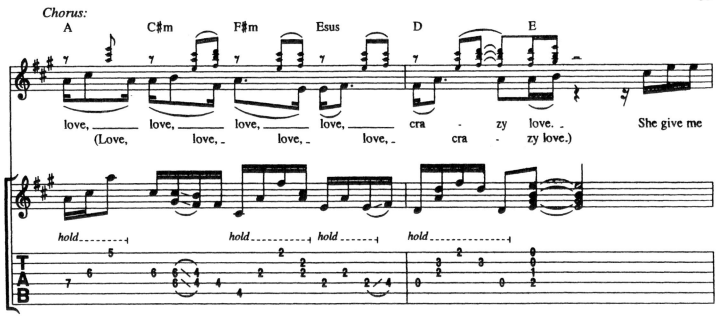

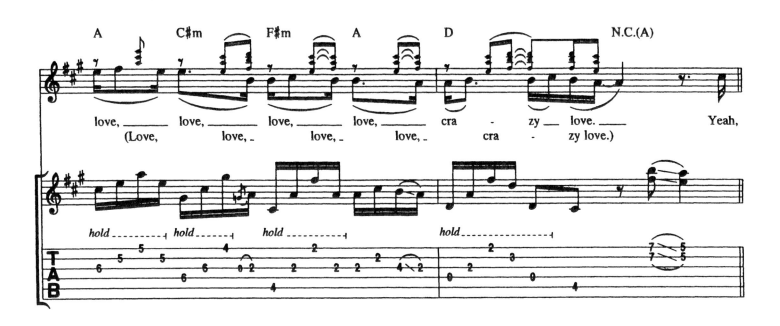

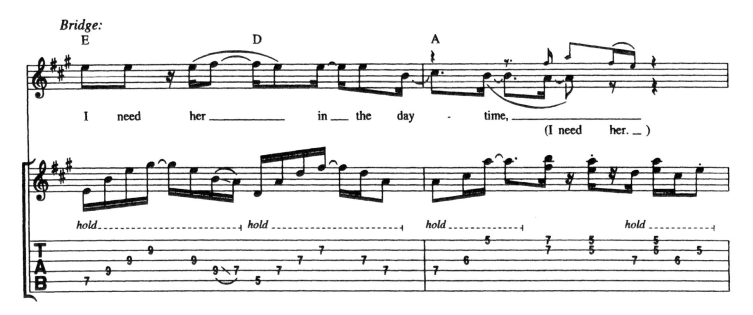

Crazy Love - 8 - 4

56

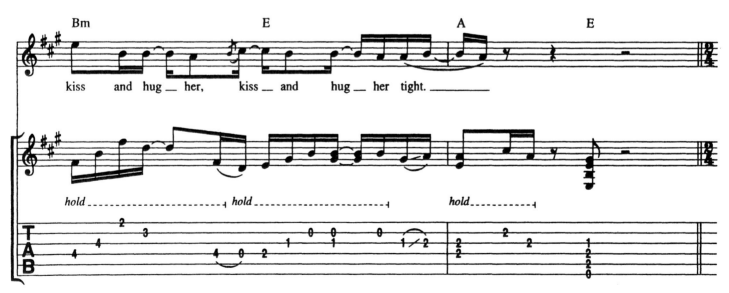

Crazy Love - 8 - 5

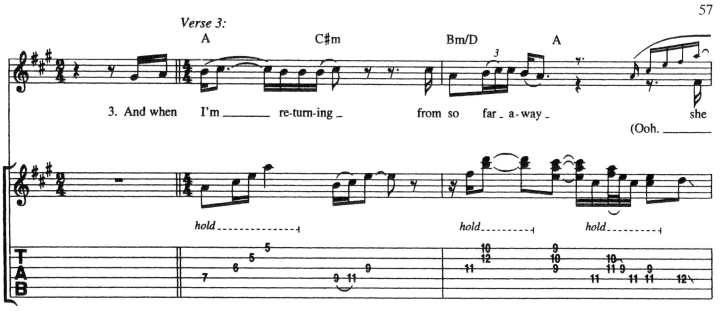

Verse 3:

3. And when I'm _____ re-turn-ing ___ from so far _ a-way _ she (Ooh. _____

gives me some __ sweet lov-in' __ bright-ens up my day. _____ Yeah, and
_____) (Ooh. _____

it makes __ me right-eous, yeah, and it makes me whole.
_____) (Ooh. _____

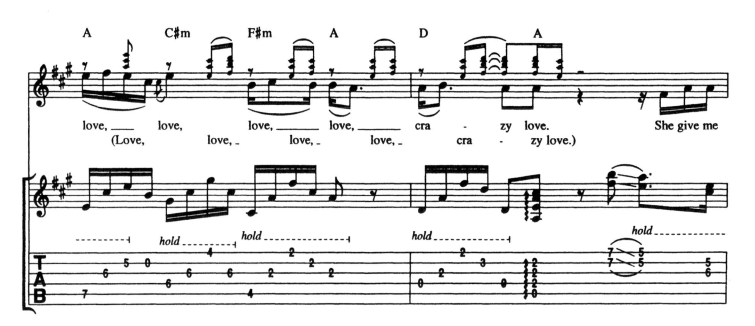

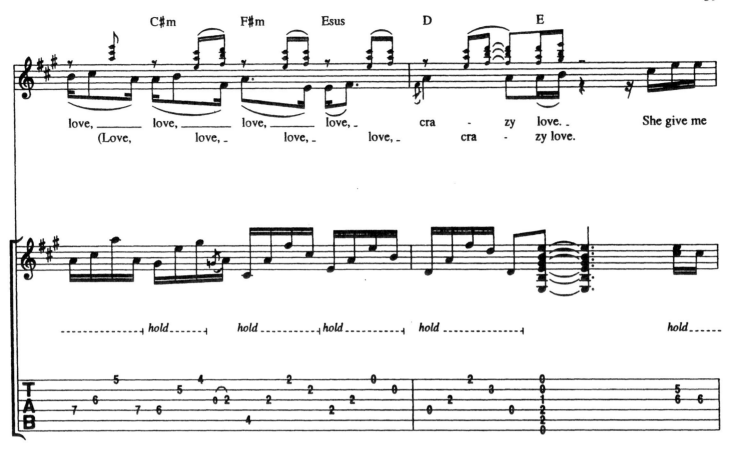

Crazy Love - 8 - 8

COME RUNNING
(Come Running to Me)

Words and Music by
VAN MORRISON

Moderately ♩ = 96

Intro:

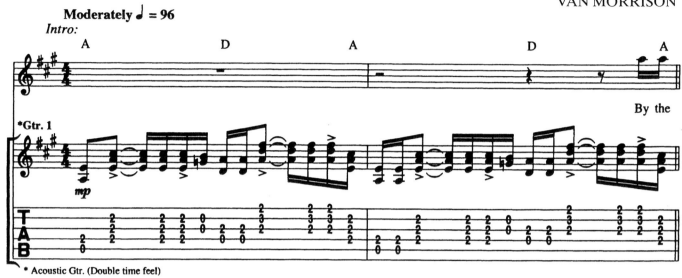

* Acoustic Gtr. (Double time feel)

Verse:

1. side of the tracks where the train goes by, __ the wind and rain will catch you, you will

2.3. *See additional lyrics*

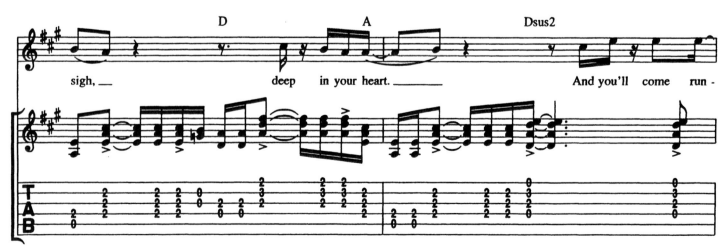

sigh, __ deep in your heart. _____ And you'll come run -

Come Running - 5 - 1

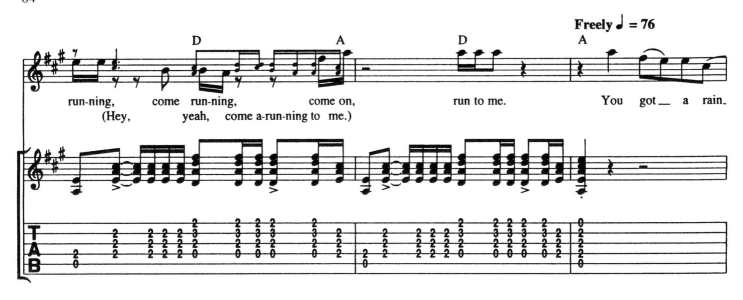

run-ning, come run-ning, come on, run to me. You got a rain
(Hey, yeah, come a-run-ning to me.)

bow if you run to me.

Verse 2:
Well you watch the train go 'round the bend;
Play in dust and dream that it will never end
Deep in your heart.
You'll come a-running to me.
You'll come a-running to me.
(To Chorus:)

Verse 3:
Kick the sand up with your heels.
You think to yourself how good it feels.
Put away all your walking shoes.
Then you come running to me.
Now you come running to me.
(To Chorus:)

MOONDANCE

Words and Music by
VAN MORRISON

66

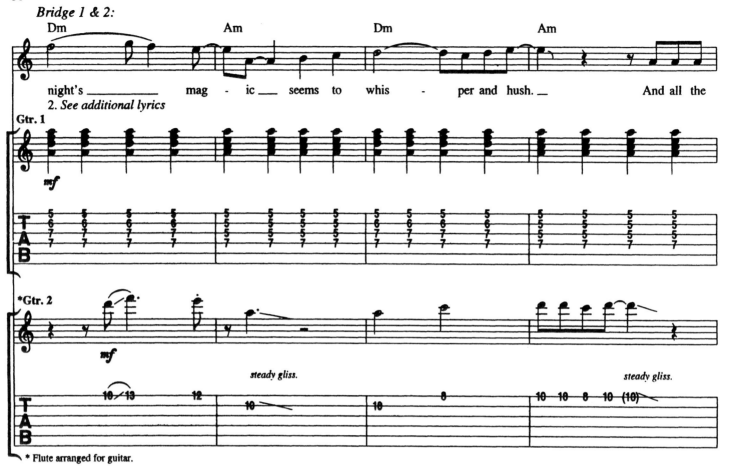

* Flute arranged for guitar.

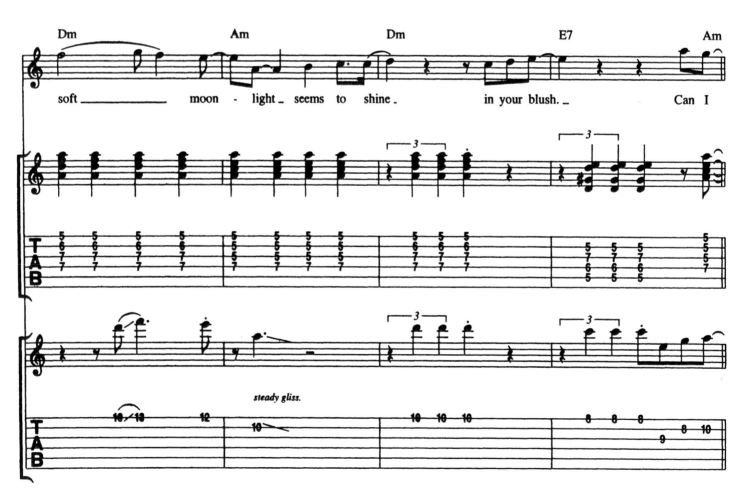

Moondance - 5 - 2

Chorus:

just have one a - more moon dance with you, my love? _ Can I _

To Coda ⊕

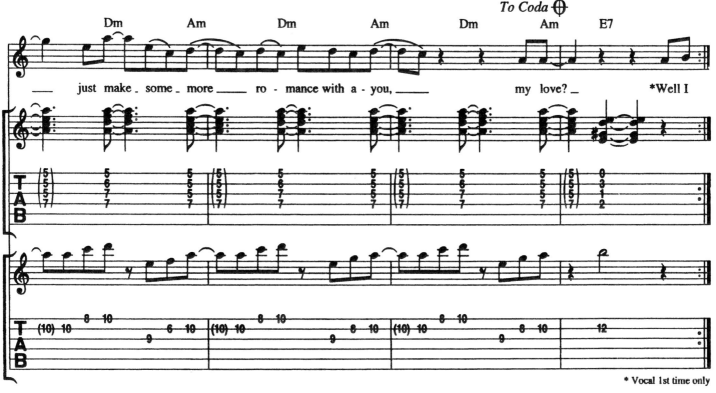

just make some more ro - mance with a - you, _ my love? _ *Well I

* Vocal 1st time only

Piano Solo:
Gtr. 2 out
Gtr. 1

Saxophone Solo:

D.S. %S al Coda

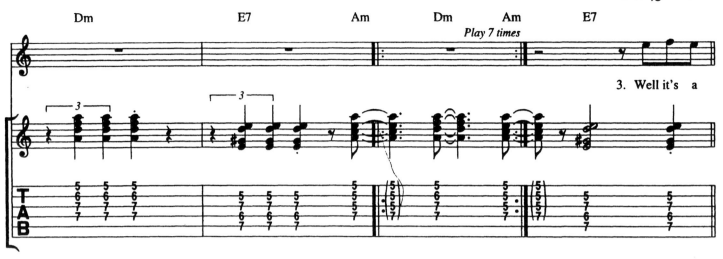

3. Well it's a

⊕ *Coda*

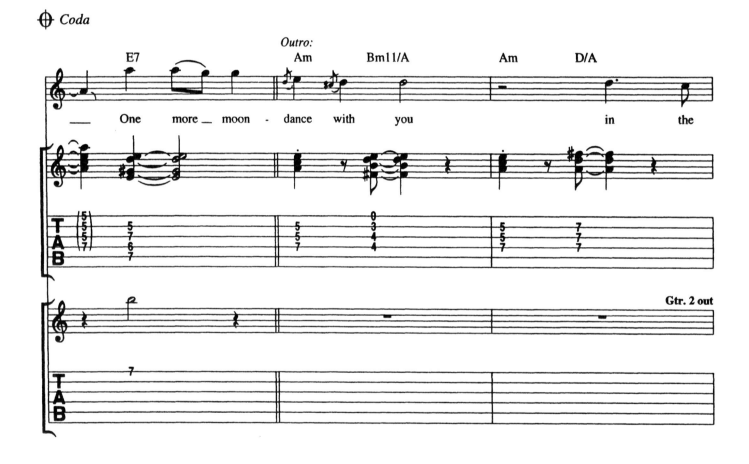

One more — moon - dance with you in the

Gtr. 2 out

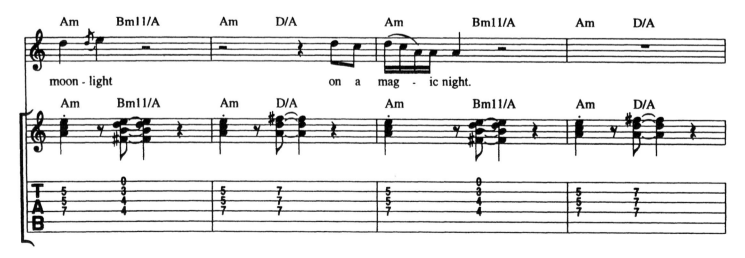

moon - light on a mag - ic night.

Verse 2:

Well I wanna make love to you tonight,
I can't wait 'til the morning has come.
And I know now the time is just right
And straight into my arms you will run.
And when you come, my heart will be waiting
To make sure that you're never alone.
There and then all my dreams will come true, dear,
There and then I will make you my own.

Bridge 2:

And everytime I touch you, you just tremble inside.
And I know how much you want me that you can't hide.

(To Chorus:)

HAVE I TOLD YOU LATELY THAT I LOVE YOU?

Words and Music by
VAN MORRISON

Have I told you late - ly_____ that I love you?_____

Have I told you there's no___ one a - bove you?___

Yeah, you fill my heart with glad - ness,___ take a - way my sad - ness.

Ease my trou - ble, that's what you do. 1. All I

Verse:

want is some of the Lord's glo - ry.____ He said

2. *(Inst. solo ad lib....*

Have I Told You Lately That I Love You? - 4 - 1

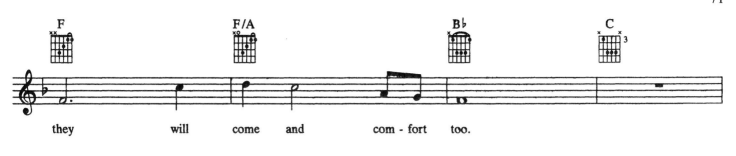

they will come and com - fort too.

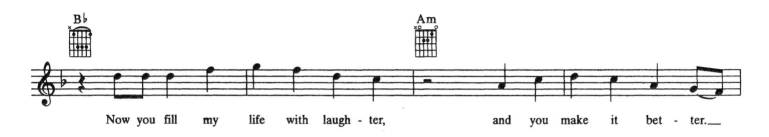

Now you fill my life with laugh - ter, and you make it bet - ter.__

Ease my trou - bles, that's what you do.

. . . end solo)

Bridge:

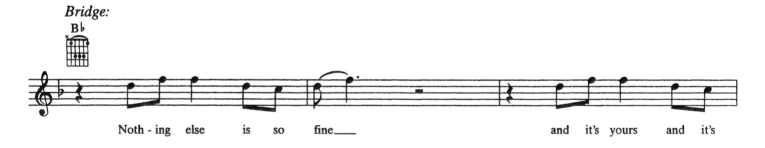

Noth - ing else is so fine__ and it's yours and it's

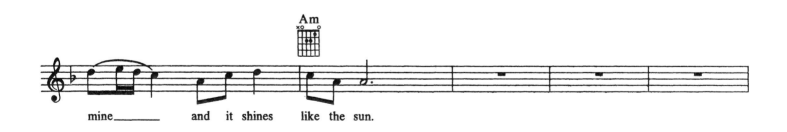

mine__ and it shines like the sun.

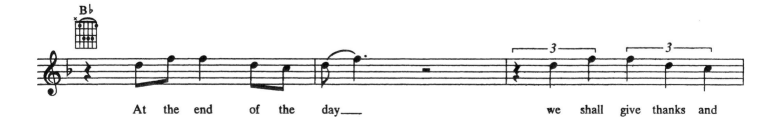

At the end of the day__ we shall give thanks and

Chorus:

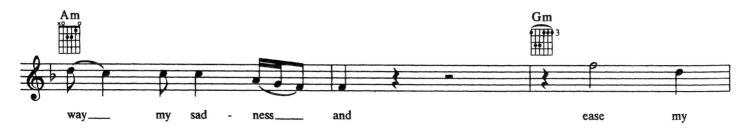

way___ my sad - ness___ and ease my

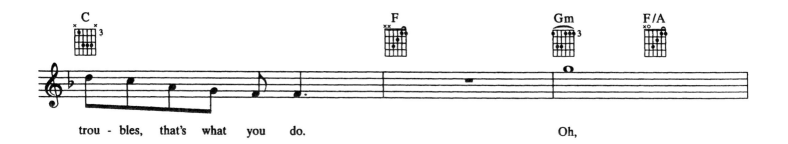

trou - bles, that's what you do. Oh,

you fill my heart with glad - ness,___ and take a -

way___ my sad - ness___ and, and you ease my trou - bles, that's what

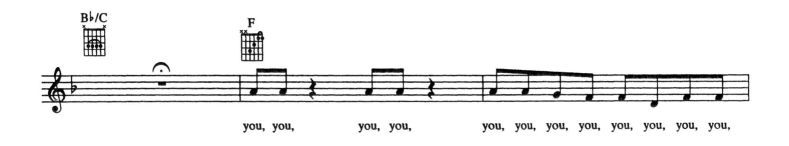

you, you, you, you, you, you, you, you, you, you, you, you,

you, you, you, you, you, you, you.

INTO THE MYSTIC

Words and Music by
VAN MORRISON

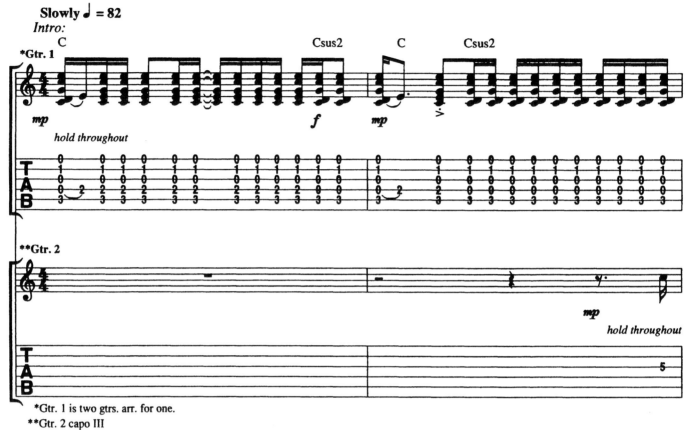

*Gtr. 1 is two gtrs. arr. for one.
**Gtr. 2 capo III
To match record key of E♭: Gtr. 1 capo III, Gtr. 2 capo VI

Into the Mystic - 14 - 1

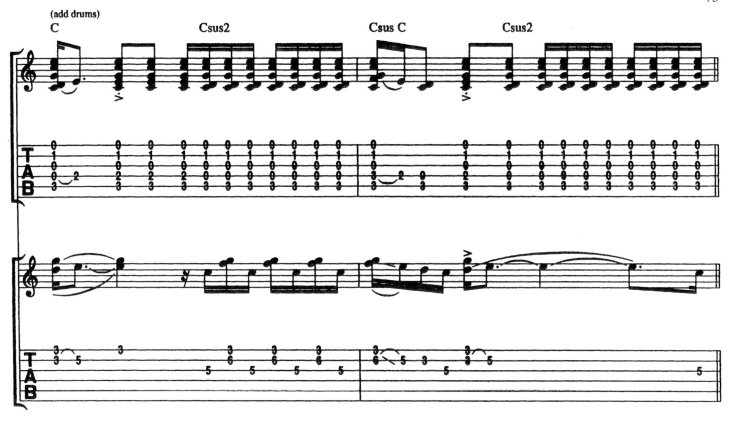

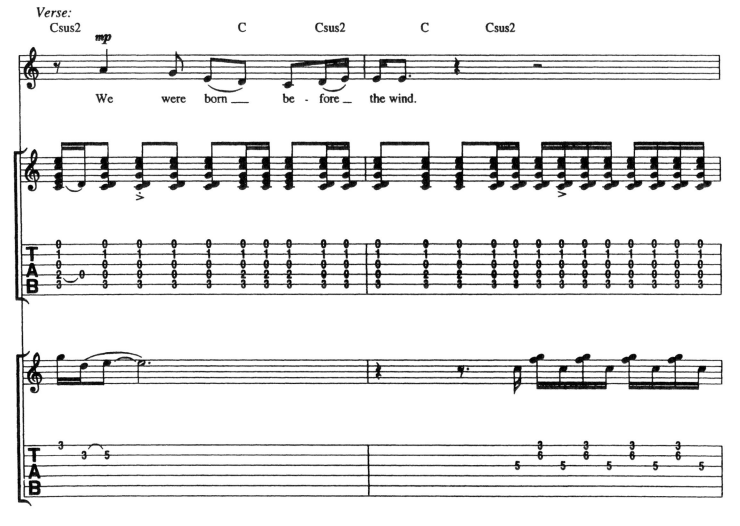

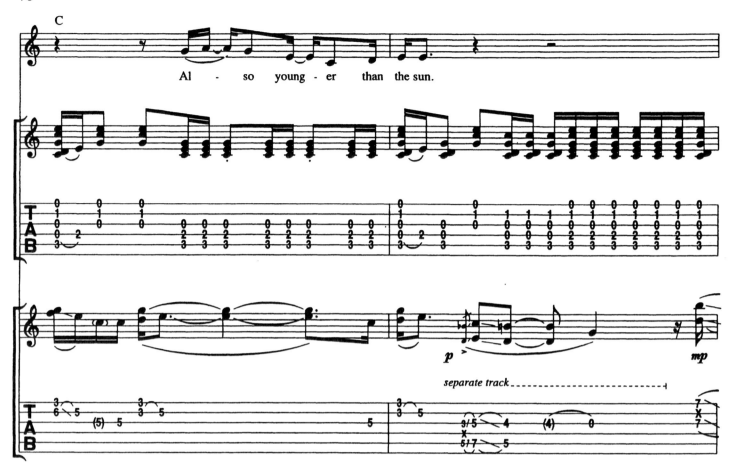

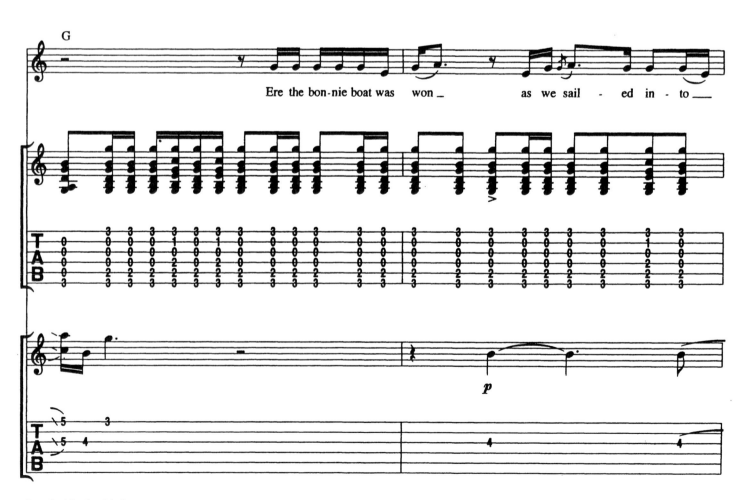

C   Csus2   C

the mys-tic.

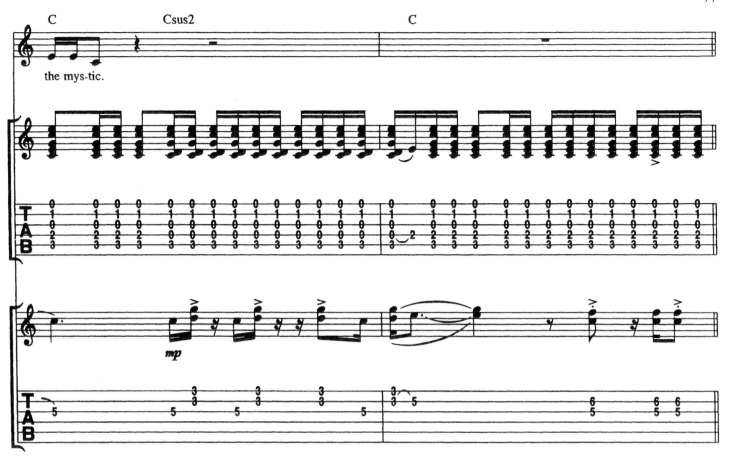

Verse:
C   Csus2

Hark, _____ now hear _____ the sail-ors cry. _____

Rhy. Fig. 1

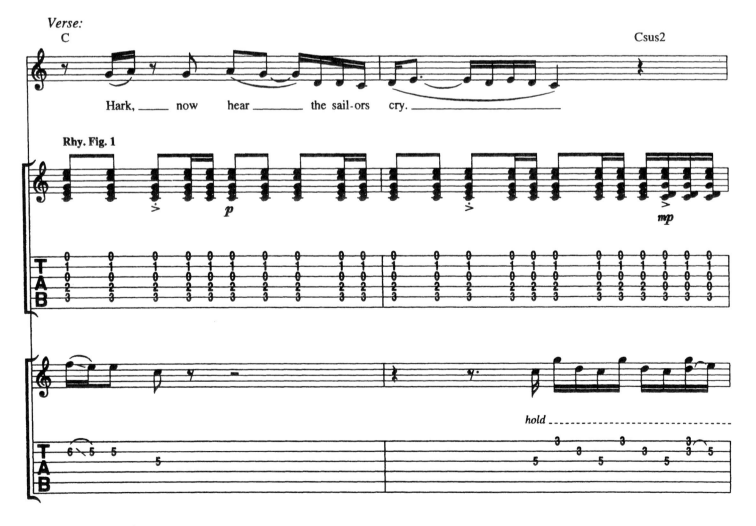

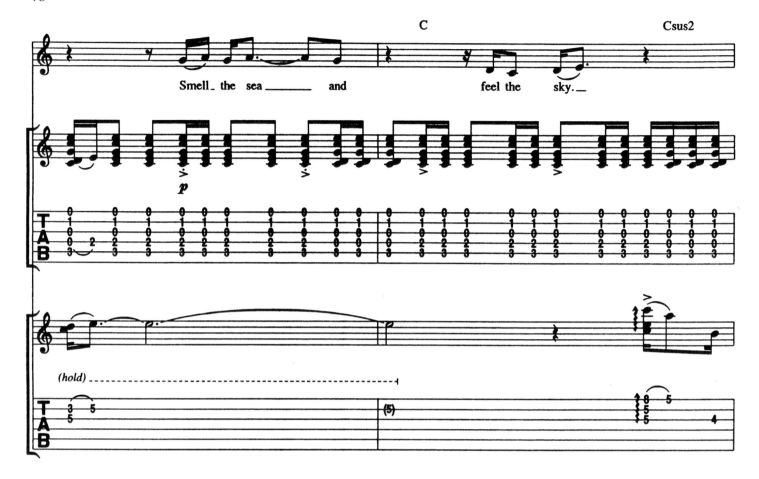

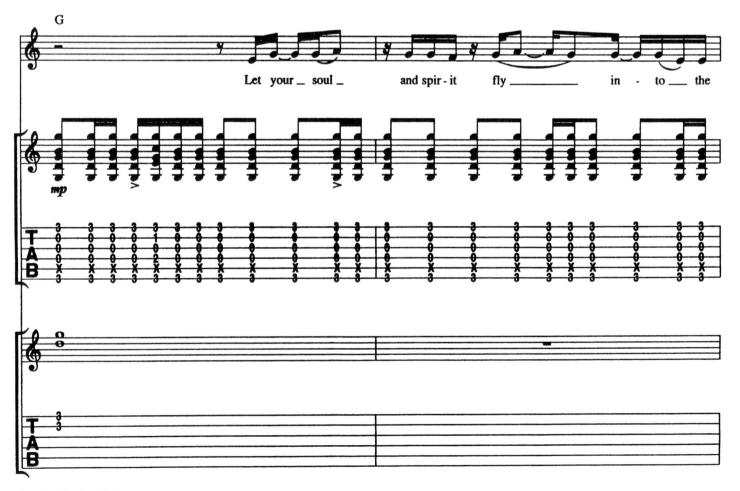

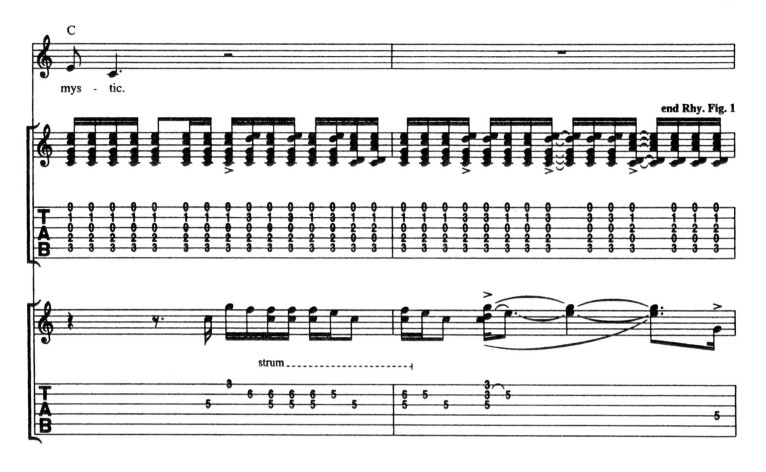

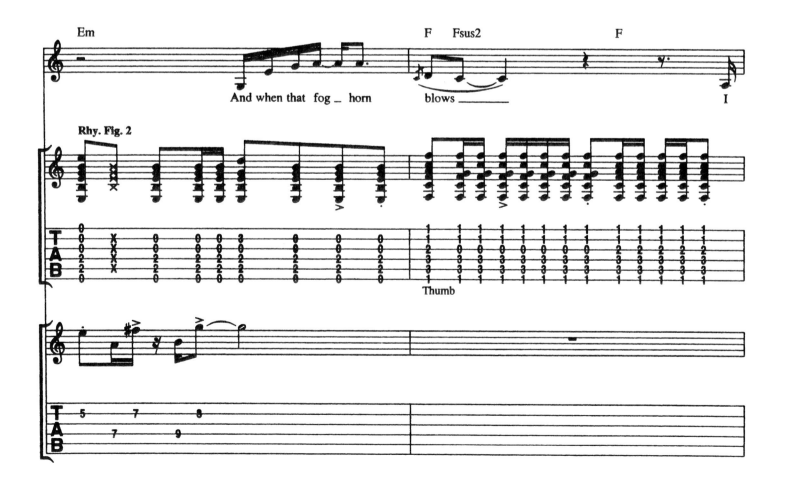

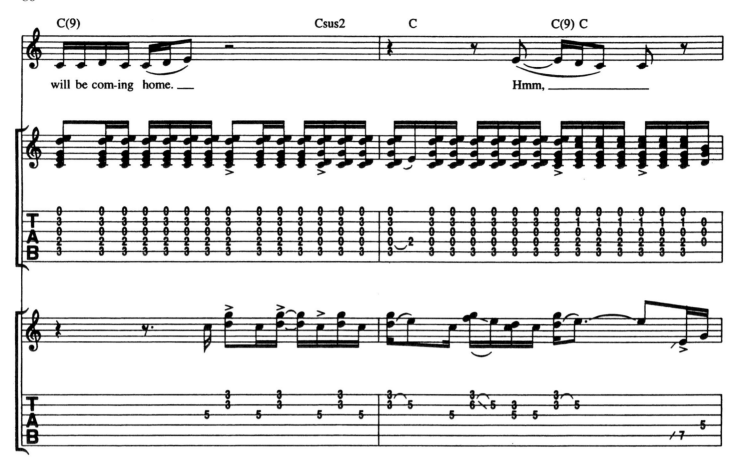

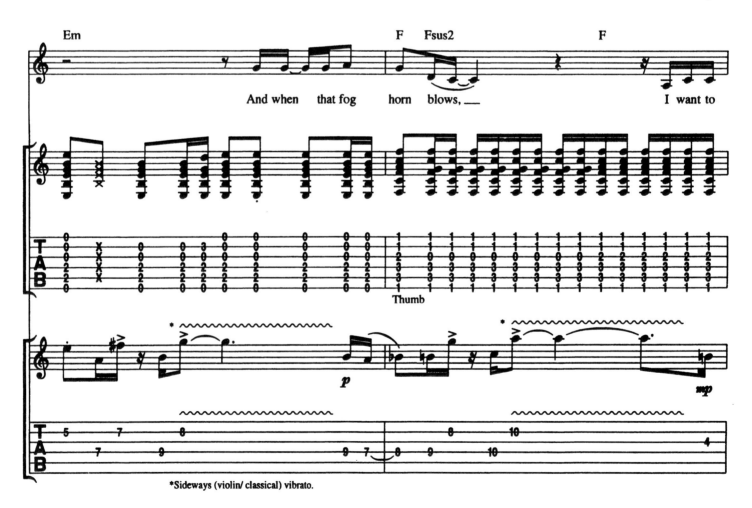

*Sideways (violin/ classical) vibrato.

And mag-nif-i-cent-ly we will float ___ in - to the

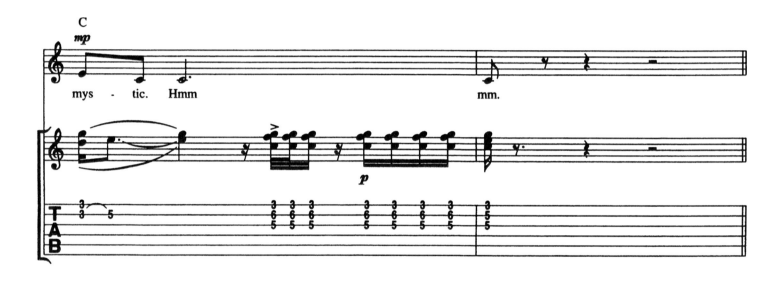

mys - tic. Hmm   mm.

Verse:
(Instrumental with alto and tenor saxes)
C
Rhy. Fig. 3

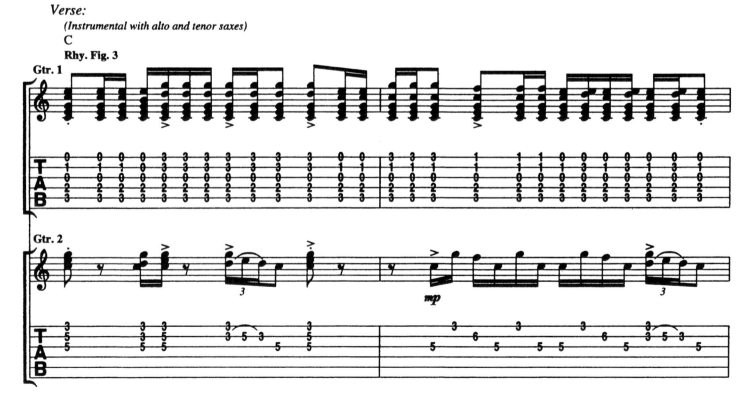

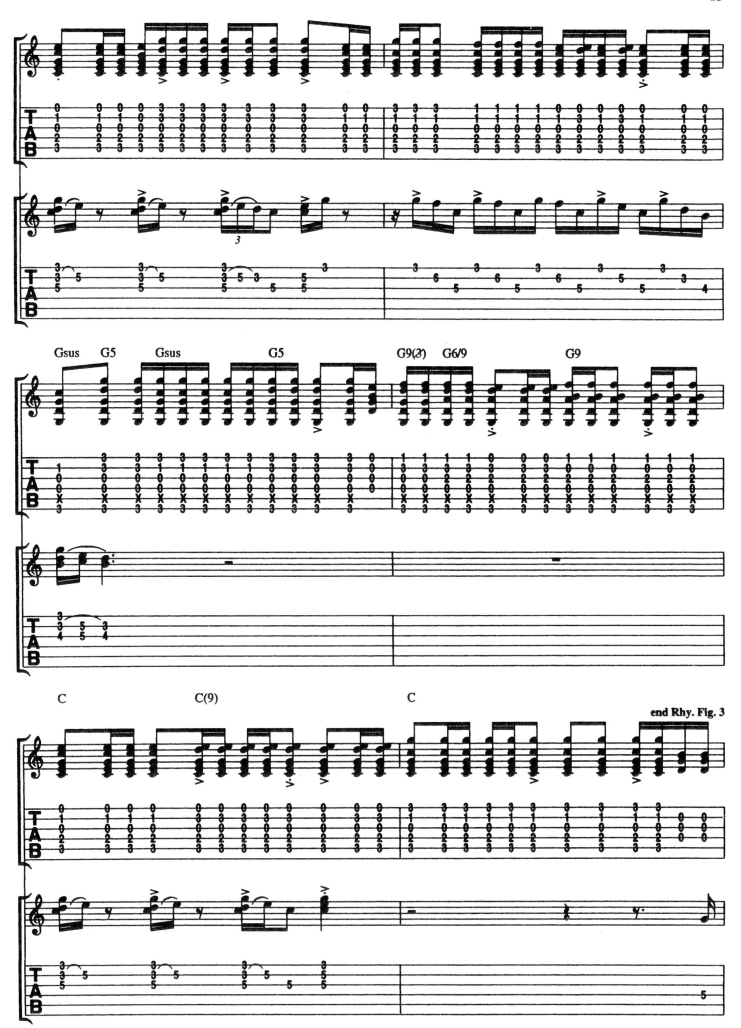

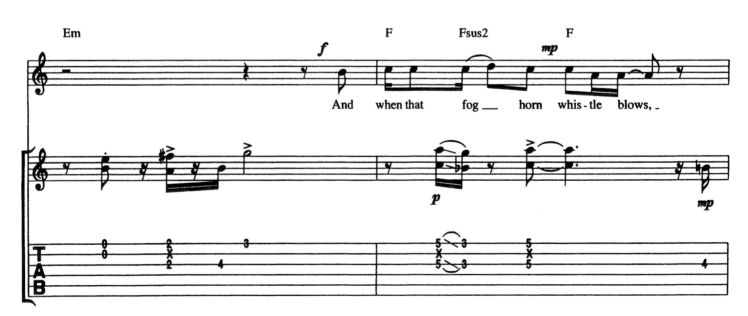

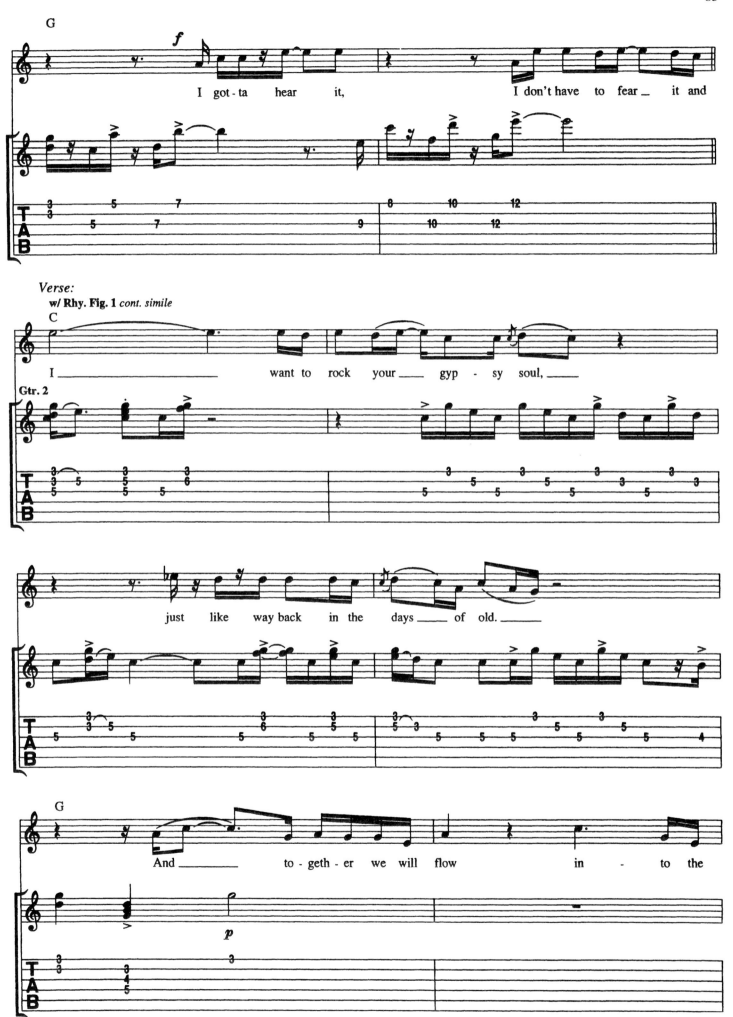

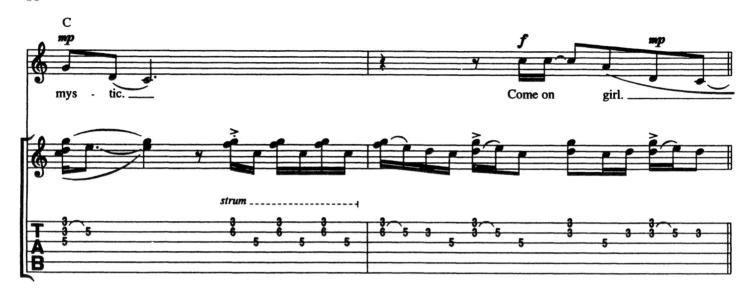

mys - tic. ____

Come on   girl. ____

Verse:
(Instrumental with horns as before)
w/ Rhy. Fig. 3 *cont'd. simile*

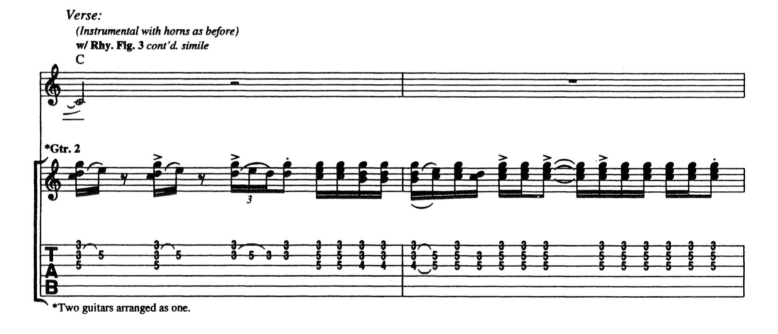

*Gtr. 2

*Two guitars arranged as one.

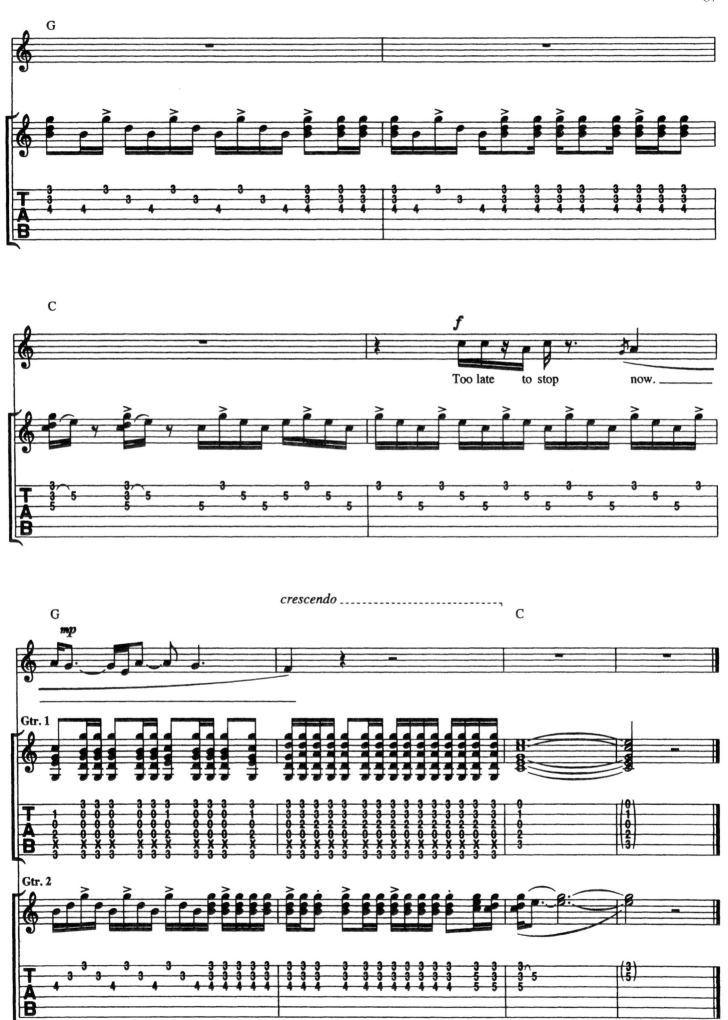

JACKIE WILSON SAID

(I'm in Heaven When You Smile)

Words and Music by
VAN MORRISON

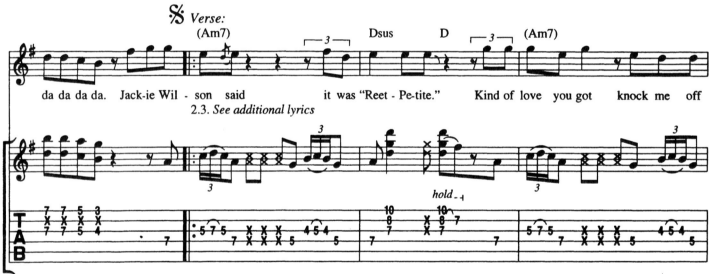

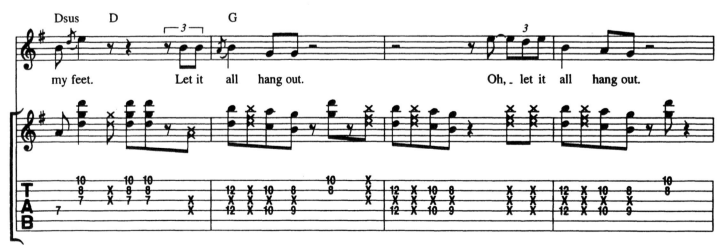

Jackie Wilson Said - 4 - 1

Jackie Wilson Said - 4 - 2

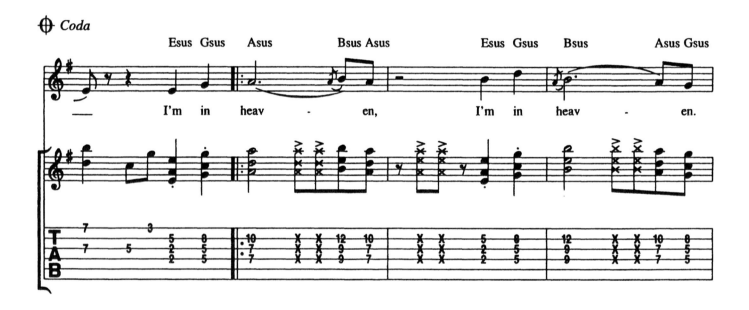

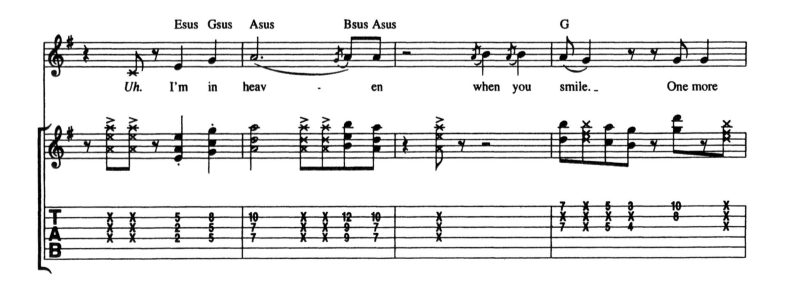

Verse 2:
And you know,
I'm so wired up.
Don't need no coffee in my cup.
Let it all hang out.
Let it all hang out.
(To Pre-Chorus:)

Verse 3:
And when you walk
Across the road,
You make my heart go
Boom-boom-boom.
Let it all hang out.
(To Verse 4:)

Verse 4:
And ev'ry time
You look that way
Honey chile, you make my day.
Let it all hang out.
Like the man said: Let it all hang out.

SWEET THING

Words and Music by
VAN MORRISON

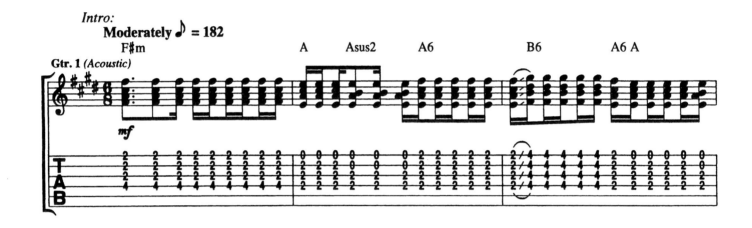

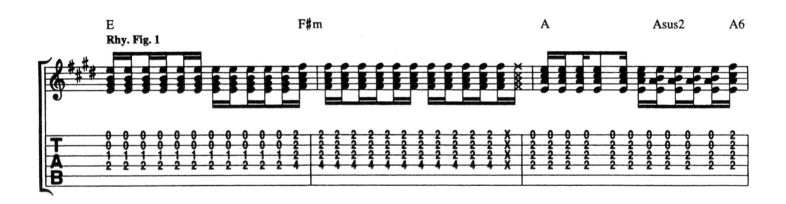

1. And I will stroll the mer-ry way and jump the
2. 3. *See additional lyrics*

Next 24 bars Verse 2 only

*Gtr. 2 ad Lib. on Verse 3 à la Verse 2.

Sweet Thing - 5 - 1

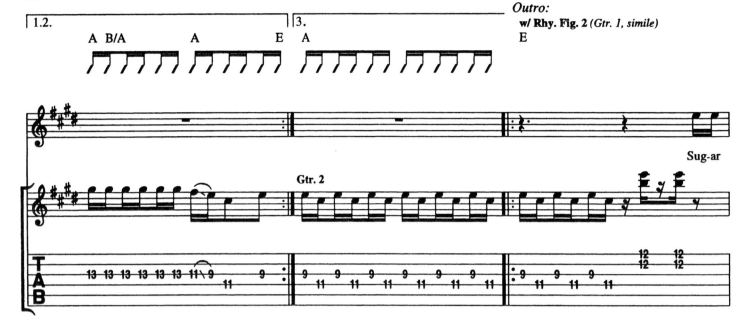

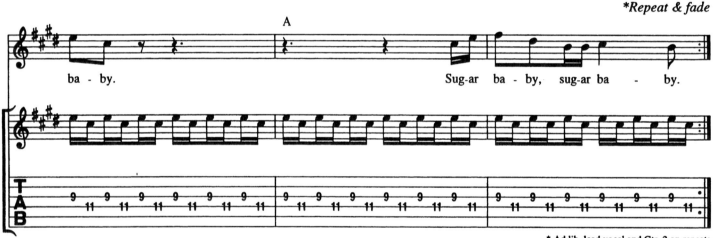

* Ad lib. lead vocal and Gtr. 2 on repeats

Verse 2:
And I shall drive my chariot down your streets and cry.
"Hey, it's me, I'm dynamite and I don't know why."
And you shall take my strongly in your arms again.
And I will not remember that I ever felt the pain.
We shall walk and talk in gardens all misty wet, misty wet with rain.
And I will never, never, never grow so old again.
(To Chorus:)

Verse 3:
And I will raise my hand up into the night-time sky.
And count the stars that's shining in your eye.
And just to dig it all not to wonder that's just fine.
And I'll be satisfied not to read in between the lines.
And I will walk and talk in gardens all wet with rain.
And I will never, ever, ever, ever grow so old again.
Oh sweet thing, sweet thing
Sugar baby with your champagne eyes
And your saint-like smile.
(To Chorus:)

WONDERFUL REMARK

Words and Music by
VAN MORRISON

Wonderful Remark - 5 - 1

98

Wonderful Remark - 5 - 2

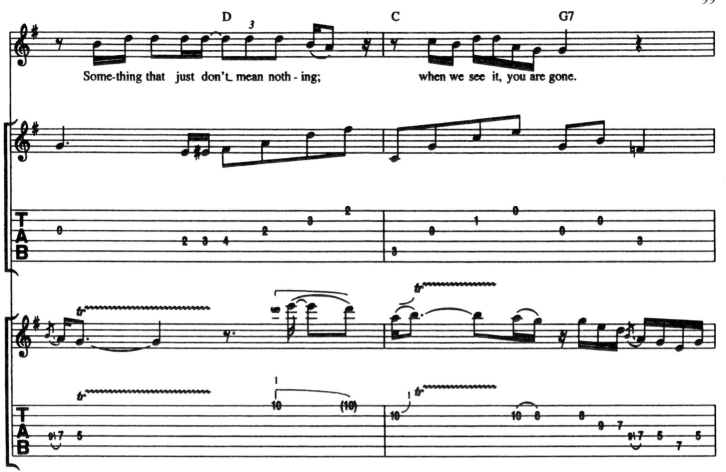

Some-thing that just don't mean noth - ing; when we see it, you are gone.

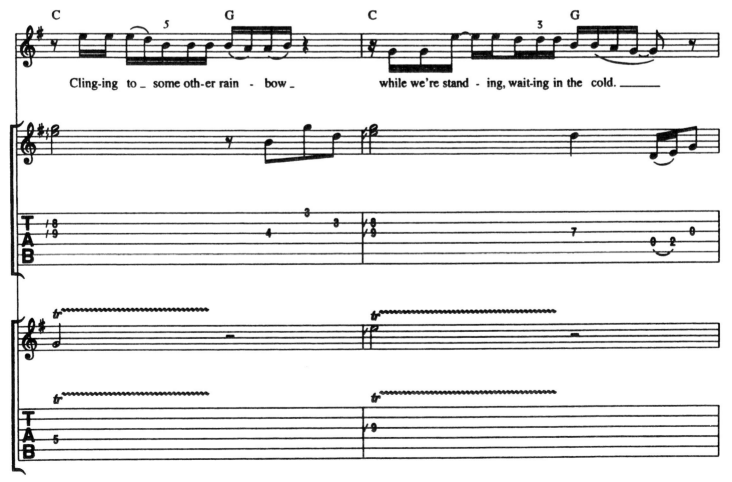

Cling-ing to _ some oth-er rain - bow _ while we're stand - ing, wait-ing in the cold. _____

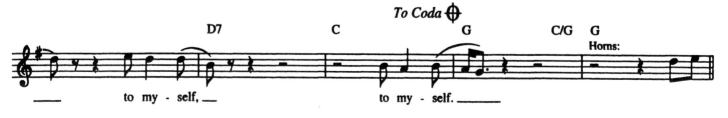

Repeat & Fade

Verse 2:

How can we listen to you
When we know your talk is cheap?
How can we ever question
Why we give more and you keep?
How can your empty laughter
Fill a room like ours with joy
When you're only playing with us
Like a child does with a toy?
How can we ever feel the freedom
Or the flame lit by the spark?
How can we ever come out even
When reality is stark?
(To Chorus:)

TUPELO HONEY

Words and Music by
VAN MORRISON

* Flute and keyboard arranged for guitar.

Tupelo Honey - 10 - 1

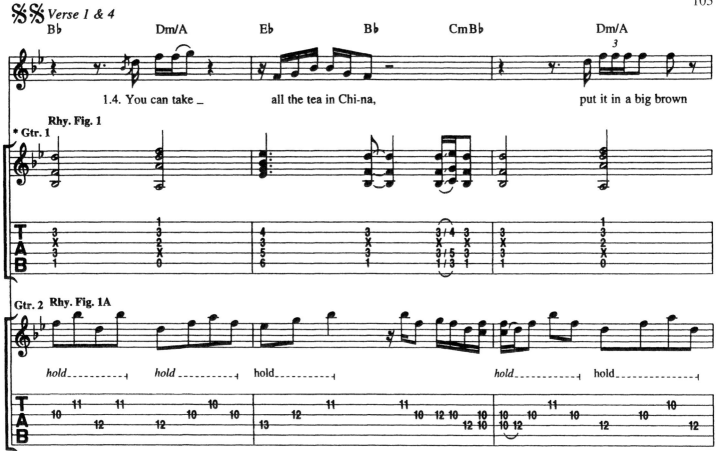

* Keyboard doubles Gtr. 1 simile throughout Verse 1.

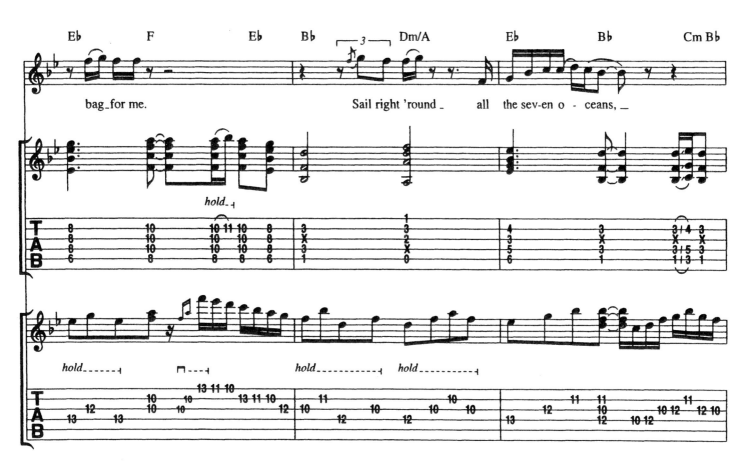

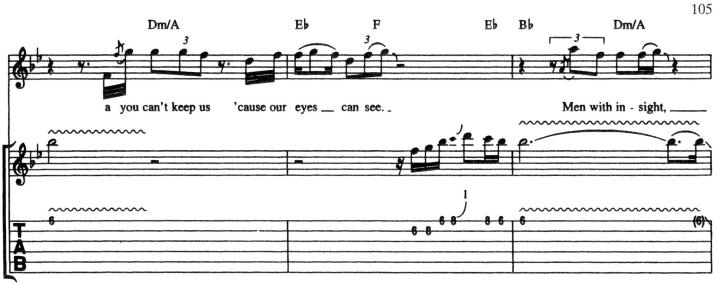

a you can't keep us 'cause our eyes ___ can see.. Men with in - sight, ____

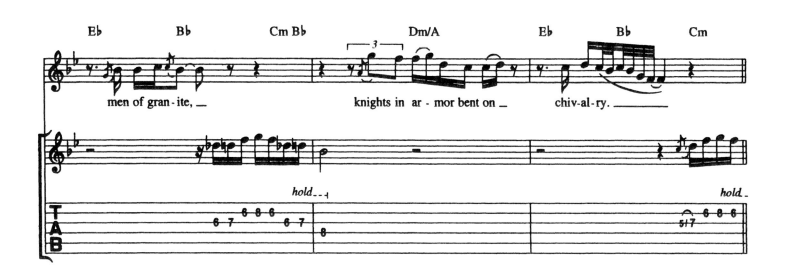

men of gran - ite, ___ knights in ar - mor bent on ___ chiv-al-ry. _____

Chorus:

She's ___ as ___ sweet ___ as ___ tu-pe-lo hon-ey, she's an an - gel of

106

* Gtrs. 1 and 2 are joined by saxophone in an exchange of melodic ideas.

Tupelo Honey - 10 - 5

Guitar Solo:

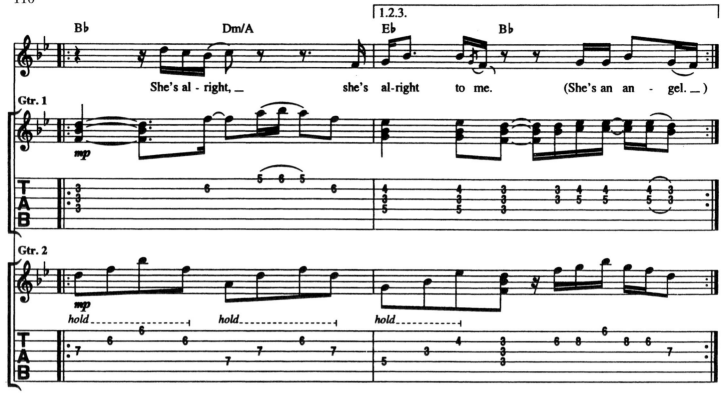

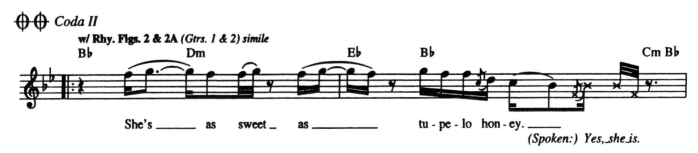

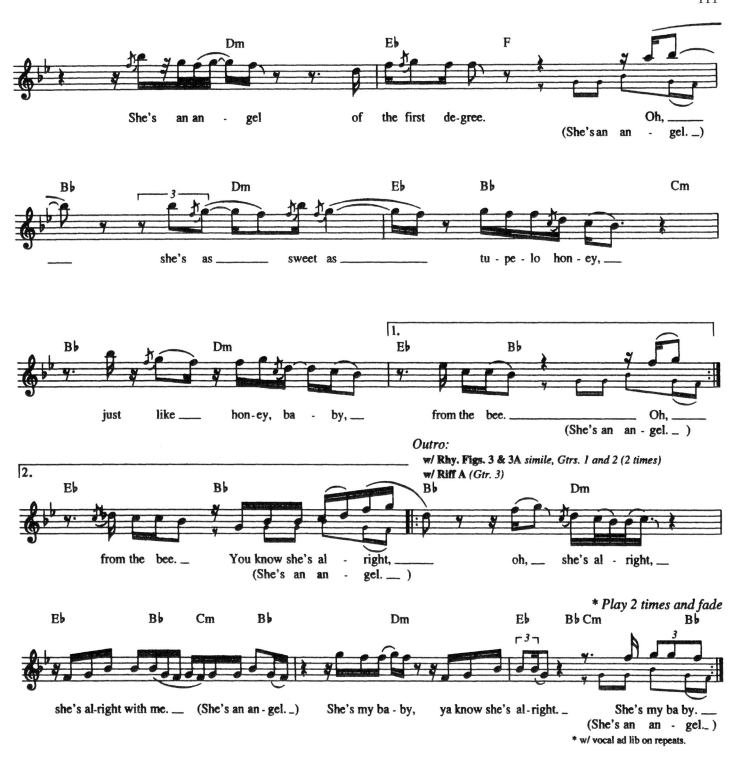

Verse 3:
You can't stop us
On the road to freedom.
You can't stop us
'Cause our eyes can see
Men with insight
Men of gran-ite
Knights in armor intent on chivalry.
(To Chorus:)

WARM LOVE

Words and Music by
VAN MORRISON

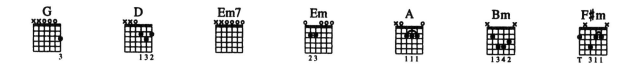

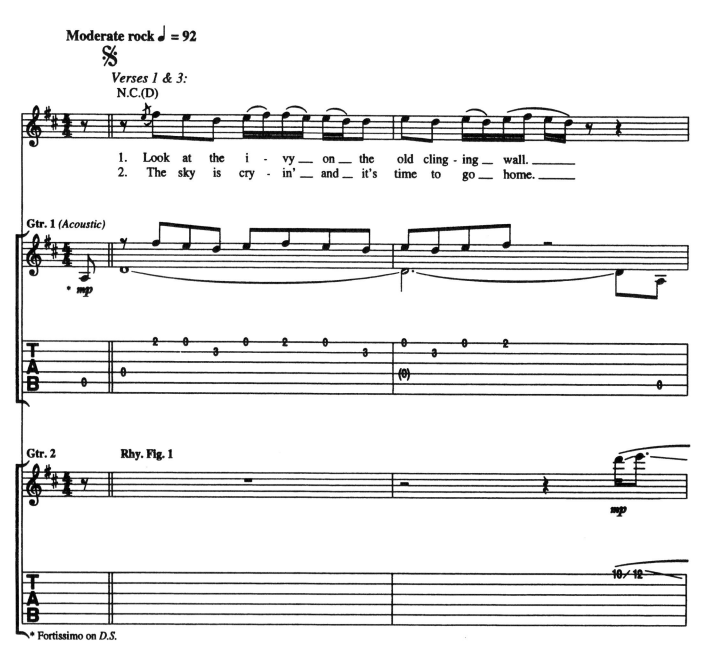

1. Look at the i - vy __ on __ the old cling - ing __ wall. _____
2. The sky is cry - in' __ and __ it's time to go __ home. _____

* Fortissimo on *D.S.*

Warm Love - 8 - 1

Look at the flow - ers ___ and the green grass so tall. ___
And we shall hur - ry ___ to the car from the foam. ___

** Secondary vocal sung on *D.S.* only.

It's not a mat - ter ___ of when push comes to shove, ___
Sit by the fire ___ and dry out our wet clothes. ___

Gtr. 1

Gtr. 2

*Gtr. 3

mp

* Woodwinds arranged for guitar.

114

Warm Love - 8 - 3

116

Bridge 3:
Inside it's warm love.
Inside it's warm love.
(To Chorus:)

WILD NIGHT

Words and Music by
VAN MORRISON

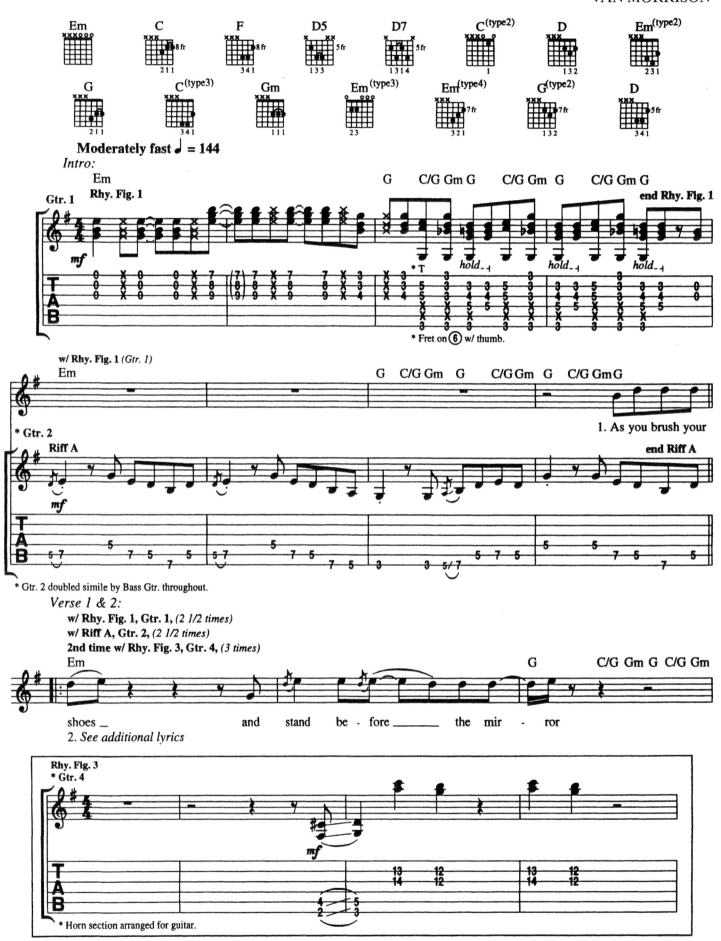

and you comb your hair   and   grab your coat and __ hat. ____

And you   walk ____   wet streets, try - in' ____ to re - mem -

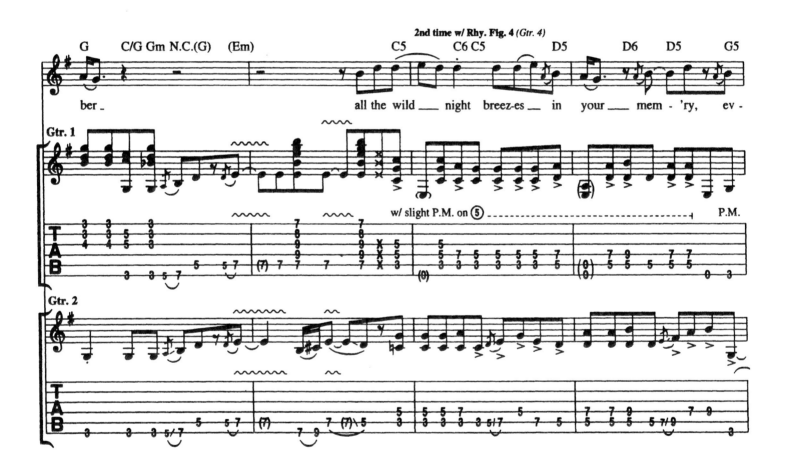

ber __   all the wild ___ night breez-es ___ in   your ____ mem - 'ry,   ev -

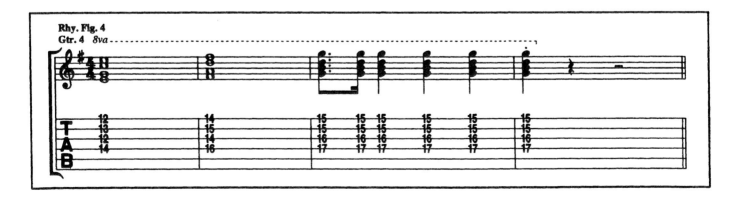

Pre-Chorus:
2nd time w/ Rhy. Fig. 5 simile, Gtr. 4 (4 times)

er. _ And ev-'ry - thing looks so com - plete _ when

w/ Rhy. Fig. 2, Gtr. 1 (2 times)
w/ Riffs B & B1 simile (2 times)

you walk-in' out ___ on the street _ and the wind catch-es your feet. and sends you fly -

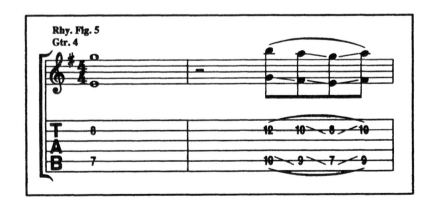

** Depress bar before striking note.   * Gtr. 1 doubled simile by horn section (Gtr. 4).

124

Wild Night - 8 - 5

* Horn section doubles Pedal Steel simile.

126

Wild Night - 8 - 7

Verse 2:

And all the girls walk by, dressed up for each other.

And the boys do the boogie-woogie on the corner of the street.

And the people passin' by just stare in wild wonder.

And the inside juke-box roars out just like thunder.

(To Pre-chorus:)

TABLATURE EXPLANATION

TAB illustrates the six strings of the guitar.
Notes and chords are indicated by the placement of fret numbers on each string.

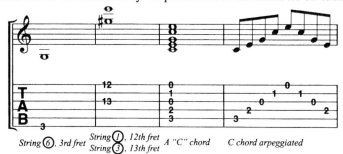

String ⑥, 3rd fret   String ①, 12th fret   A "C" chord   C chord arpeggiated
String ③, 13th fret

BENDING NOTES

Half Step:
Play the note and bend string one half step (one fret).

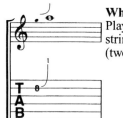

Whole Step:
Play the note and bend string one whole step (two frets).

Slight Bend/ Quarter-Tone Bend:
Play the note and bend string sharp.

Prebend and Release:
Play the already-bent string, then immediately drop it down to the fretted note.

Bend and Release:
Play the note and bend to the next pitch, then release to the original note. Only the first note is attacked.

PICK DIRECTION

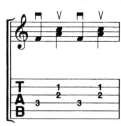

Downstrokes and Upstrokes:
The downstroke is indicated with this symbol (⊓) and the upstroke is indicated with this (V).

ARTICULATIONS

Hammer On:
Play the lower note, then "hammer" your finger to the higher note. Only the first note is plucked.

Pull Off:
Play the higher note with your first finger already in position on the lower note. Pull your finger off the first note with a strong downward motion that plucks the string—sounding the lower note.

Palm Mute:
The notes are muted (muffled) by placing the palm of the pick hand lightly on the strings, just in front of the bridge.

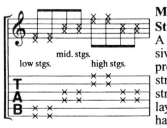

Muted Strings:
A percussive sound is produced by striking the strings while laying the fret hand across them.

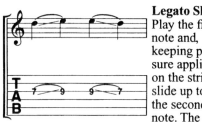

Legato Slide:
Play the first note and, keeping pressure applied on the string, slide up to the second note. The diagonal line shows that it is a slide and not a hammer-on or a pull-off.

HARMONICS

Natural Harmonic:
A finger of the fret hand lightly touches the string at the note indicated in the TAB and is plucked by the pick producing a bell-like sound called a harmonic.

RHYTHM SLASHES

Strum Marks/ Rhythm Slashes:
Strum with the indicated rhythm pattern. Strum marks can be located above the staff or within the staff.

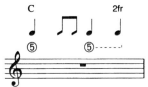

Single Notes with Rhythm Slashes:
Sometimes single notes are incorporated into a strum pattern. The circled number below is the string and the fret number is above.

Artificial Harmonic:
Fret the note at the first TAB number, lightly touch the string at the fret indicated in parens (usually 12 frets higher than the fretted note), then pluck the string with an available finger or your pick.